D1743907

What
the
Bible
Means
to
Me

Compiled by
BASIL C. MOWLL

LONDON
PICKERING & INGLIS LTD

PICKERING & INGLIS LTD
29 LUDGATE HILL, LONDON EC4M 7BP
26 BOTHWELL STREET, GLASGOW G2 6PA

ISBN 0 7208 0300 4

Cat. No. 01/2216

First published 1974
Reprinted   1976

Printed in Great Britain by
Lowe & Brydone Printers Limited, Thetford, Norfolk

Contents

Preface

The enemies of God's Truth by subtle infiltration into our church life have done much to destroy our nation's past belief in the Bible as the Word of God. The present spiritual and moral state of our country clearly shows the terrible folly of our departure from the Word of God.

If this Book is true as the contributors of these articles all believe, then the one and only escape from national disaster is to repent of our folly and turn once again to the reliability and authority of this unique Book, the only one in the whole world which makes the stupendous claim that it is the Word of God. Most of these articles have recently appeared in the *Lymington Times* by the kind permission of the editor of that paper. I warmly thank him and all who have so willingly contributed to this united testimony to the great value of the Bible.

I would close this preface by quoting the words with which Dr. Alexander Robertson closes his book, *The Papal Conquest*, written in 1909 as a warning to our nation, and I would thankfully acknowledge the kind permission to do this by the publishers Messrs Marshall, Morgan & Scott. Here is Dr. Robertson's closing appeal:

'I would plead with my countrymen everywhere to reinstate the Bible in its old place of sovereignty in their homes and in their hearts, not only realizing it to be the most marvellous book of instruction and culture in the whole range of literature, but as the Living Word of the Living God; and so to read it and study it morning by morning, and evening by evening, so as to find in its every book JESUS CHRIST, to exhibit whom every book was written.'

BASIL C. MOWLL

Acknowledgements

We would like to thank Dr. Billy Graham for permission to use extracts from his booklet *Our Bible*; Hodder & Stoughton Limited, London for permission to reprint the extract from *The Way I See It* by Cliff Richard; also the extract from *Crypts of Power* by Sir Kenneth Grubb, K.C.M.G.; the editor of *Practical Christianity*, the magazine of The Officers' Christian Union, for permission to reprint articles by Major K. Hedges, M.B., CH.B., D.T.M., R.A.M.C., and Victor Pollard.

Indulgence is begged in case of failure to reach any other author or holder of copyrighted portions.

Cover Photographs—
Top left: Stan Smith (*Copyright Tennis World*)
Top right: Cliff Richard (*Copyright Dezo Hoffmann*)
Bottom Left: Victor Pollard (*Copyright Sport & General*)
Bottom centre: Dr. Andrew Michael Ramsay
                              (*Copyright Baron Studios Ltd.*)
Bottom right: Dr. Billy Graham

Queen Elizabeth The Queen Mother

Queen Elizabeth The Queen Mother sent this message to an exhibition, 'The Festival of Britain', when it was opened at the Central Hall, Westminster, on Saturday, 1st September, 1951.

'I am most happy to send my good wishes for the success of the exhibition which the World Evangelical Alliance has arranged for the Festival year, together with my congratulations on maintaining the vision and enterprise which have always been a characteristic of the Alliance for more than one hundred years. That cherished inheritance which we call "The British way of life" has its source and inspiration in the great ideals of Christianity. It is fitting indeed that we should take this opportunity of showing how the life of our nation has long been influenced by our faith, and moulded by the Bible.

I can truly say that the King and I long to see the Bible back where it ought to be, as a guide and comfort in the homes and lives of our people. From our experience we know what the Bible can mean for personal life. I hope this exhibition will help our nation to be Christian in fact, as well as in name, and so to play its full part in leading the world towards righteousness and peace.'

Dr. Andrew Michael Ramsay

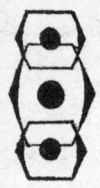

Former Archbishop of Canterbury

Extract from an address given by the Archbishop of Canterbury, 23rd June 1970.

We are meeting at a time of great encouragement. It is encouraging to find what immense interest the Bible still arouses. The excitement caused by the publication of the complete New English Bible is one sign of that.

The proclamation of the message of the Bible in the modern world must always be in the context of a Christian community which is really alive—alive in the simplicity and sincerity of its worship of God, alive in the reality of God, alive in the reality of authentic unselfish fellowship between its members and alive also in its outgoing service of the world beyond.

All biblical teaching boils down to the preaching of Jesus who is Himself in completeness, the Word proclaimed in the Old Testament, the Word proclaimed by the apostles.

In bringing the message of the Bible home today we do not only show them Jesus as Lord of the contemporary community. We also show them God as alive and active in the world around us. Now it is just this that is so often hard for people to realise and hard for us to convey. The world around us is so full of disorder and disillusionment, grief, division and frustration that sensitive people ask 'Where is God?' 'What is God doing?' Part of 'the death of God' talk means, I think, a kind of frustrated feeling. 'Can God be doing anything in this world that seems to be in such a mess?' 'Is God asleep?' 'Has God gone away?' Now what is our answer to that feeling of frustration, the feeling that God is absent? Is it not our answer to recover from the Scriptures one of the great biblical doctrines which we have perhaps rather soft-pedalled and shrunk from, namely the doctrine of the Divine judgement. God is not absent from the contemporary world today. God is present in the contemporary world; but He is present first as judge.

When a world turns its back upon God's laws calamities do happen, and calamities will go on happening; and that is indeed a part of the message of the Bible. An unrepenting world is a world, bringing calamity upon itself. 'So He gave them their heart's desire.' He let them have what, in their folly, they wanted to have; 'So He gave them their heart's desire and sent leanness withal into their souls.' Let it be known that God is present in judgement. The moment it is grasped that God is present in judgement, it is also grasped that God, present in judgement, is never present in judgement alone. He is also present in mercy, compassion, forgiveness, for the truth of God is the steadfastness of the God who both judges and raises up, both punishes and loves and saves.

When we are faithful we still go on finding that 'The Word is living, active, and sharper than any two-edged sword, piercing even to the dividing of bones and marrow', and exposing all to Him with whom we have to do.

Professor Norman Anderson
O.B.E., LL.D., F.B.A.

*Director of the Institute of Advanced
Legal Studies, and Professor of Oriental
Laws, in the University of London*

It is difficult, if not impossible, to say what the Bible means to me in a few words. Others have, no doubt, borne their testimony to the way in which they find teaching, guidance, encouragement and correction as they turn, day by day, to its pages. So I shall concentrate on a single point—which is, I think, basic in my experience: namely, the inter-relation of the Bible and Christ Himself, or God's Word written and living.

We are not bibliolaters. We do not in any sense worship the Bible. Our worship must always be directed solely to God as revealed in Jesus Christ. But how do we know who Jesus was, what He taught and did, how and why He died, and the transcendent fact of His resurrection? Primarily, of course, through the Bible. And it is important to notice that this is true quite apart from any theory of inspiration. To give a single instance: there is excellent evidence that the basic Christian 'tradition' to which St. Paul refers in the beginning in I Corinthians 15—about the death burial and resurrection of Christ— can be reliably traced back to within some five years of the actual event. And even when he wrote that letter, some twenty years later, the greater part of five hundred witnesses to the resurrection—let alone the life and teaching of Christ—were still alive to confirm, or deny, what he wrote.

So the Bible leads us straight to the 'Jesus of history' as well as the 'Christ of faith'. But He, in his turn, gives His authority to the Bible. It is inescapable, in the Gospel records, that Jesus Himself accepted the Old Testament as divinely authoritative. This emerges time after time, in all sorts of contexts—and, indeed, in every part of the Gospels. He also clearly stated that the promised Holy Spirit would bring His teaching to the remembrance of His disciples and lead them on into a deeper understanding. This covers, by implication, the Gospels and Epistles which were to form the corpus of the New Testament.

As a would-be scholar, the Bible cannot speak to me with authority unless I am convinced of its reliability and inspiration. I find this conviction in the authority of the incarnate Son of God Himself—however many superficial difficulties there may appear to be. And the fact that the message of this book—written by so many different writers over hundreds of years—is one and the same, from Genesis to Revelation, confirms its inspiration in my personal experience.

The Venerable L. J. Ashton
C.B., Q.H.C.

Chaplain-in-Chief, Royal Air Force

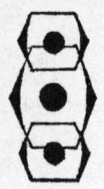

For me, as for most people, this Book has meant something different at different times in my life. I suppose it was in Sunday School and as a young schoolboy that I made my first acquaintance with the Bible. On Sundays, week by week, we learned short texts and listened to Bible stories. In school we were required to learn, presumably as literature, various passages such as Isaiah 55:

> 'Ho, everyone that thirsteth,
> come ye to the waters . . .'

and 1 Corinthians 13:

> 'Though I speak with the tongues of men
> and of angels, and have not charity . . .'

I never regarded all this as any more than a school chore, occasionally flickering to life with an exciting and bloodthirsty Old Testament story.

It was in my mid teens when I first became aware of the claims of Christ, and my faltering decision to follow Him meant that the Bible ceased to be merely paper and ink; for me its pages began to unfold the pattern of God's revelation and very dimly I began to see a little of what God has done.

In those early days the real treasures of the Word of God were first opened up for me by the ministry of a deeply spiritual vicar whose sermons and teaching were eloquent and simple expositions of the Word, and he saw to it that we were nourished by the sacred writings.

It follows that I began to read the Book for myself. I found the Scripture Union notes alone were not sufficient. Without further guidance I read long chapters, beginning at Genesis I, persevering through difficult passages, absorbed in the narrative stories, here and there perplexed and parched, but finally arriving at the New Testament, and I well remember the delight with which I read through the whole of St. John's Gospel one Christmas afternoon.

From the Bible I moved on to books about the Bible, always returning to this, the Book of books, and learning little by little to read it in a more satisfactory and intelligent way. At first my untutored and simple mind accepted it with a literalism that was naive. 4004 B.C. stood in the margin of the Authorised Version as the date of the creation, and this I accepted without question.

Later critical study in no way disturbed my faith but in fact quickened my interest and I found the Book more fascinating. The underlying documents, its mythology and history and prophecy, its parables and poetry and letters, all these things opened up seemingly limitless horizons and never-dying inspiration. My slight reading of archaeology and several visits to the Holy Land brought the dead past to life and made the people of the Book understandably human and utterly contemporary instead of being shadowy figures of a distant age.

Here God speaks as we respond imaginatively, discriminately and sympathetically to His word. Here we find divine delight, our understanding of history is enlarged, our consciences are educated, and in the richness of this Book we find the way of salvation and sanctification and the hope of eternal life—for here we find the Living Word, Jesus, the Saviour of the world and the Master of men.

That is what the Bible means to me—so great a Book because it points to so great a Person.

Cecil F. Baker,
F.A.I.C.S.

Mayor of Eastbourne three years

I had the remarkably good fortune to be born into a keen Christian family and to have parents who believed the teaching of the Bible, and understood it to be the Word of God and a guide to life not only for Sundays but also for every day of the week. This great faith which was the essence of their existence was passed on to their seven children, who have sought to follow their excellent example. The Bible contains directions for a way of life which is opposed to almost everything that is taken for granted today, and if followed, leads to happiness, peace, contentment and serenity.

My wife and I read our Bible together every day and profit greatly by its sound and profound advice and guidance. It is not only a day to day help but it also gives assurance for the future as it teaches the Christian that this world is not the end of his existence but that he has a glorious future in the life hereafter.

I became a Christian as a teenager, and for more than forty years since then I have proved the power of God, the truth of the teaching of the Bible, and the sustaining grace it gives in professional life and private life, in my recreation (I was captain of the Eastbourne Hockey Club for ten years and am still its President), in war and in peace and I am eternally grateful to my parents for their early teaching and to my wife for her constant support and fellowship in the Christian life. Perhaps I might be permitted to say that in three years as Mayor of Eastbourne I have found my faith to be the greatest possible help and support.

Major W. F. Batt,
M.B.E., D.L., J.P.

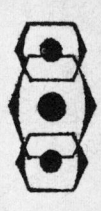

Several years as an Army officer taught me two things which helped me to become a Christain. The first is that to ignore or disobey one's Commander's orders is disastrous. The second thing is that many of the rules for officers were in a book which one was expected to learn and obey. It made sense to me, therefore when a preacher said, 'There are only two ways of life and both are described in the Bible. "All we like sheep have gone astray: we have turned every one to his own way." That is going your own way. The other way is described by Jesus Christ, "Follow Me", that is going God's way. Which way are are you going?' That evening I prayed and told Jesus that I wanted to start following Him, and asked Him to guide me. I started to re-read the Bible, and as far as I could, to do what it says, and to leave the consequences to God. Forty years experience of this has proved that the Bible is indeed God's instruction book for life, and to try to live without it leads to disaster, in the same way as ignoring the maker's handbook of one's new car. God has designed us to live by a set of absolute laws revealed in the Bible. The cause of much of the confusion, frustration and lostness and breakdown in the lives of people is that they are trying to live in God's world without the Maker's handbook, and to make up their own rules. When a person prays and tells Jesus that he knows he has been wrong and puts himself into the hands of Jesus, then Jesus accepts him, as He has promised.

As one begins to study the Bible and to obey it, God guides and helps one, and life begins to make sense.

A Borough Engineer

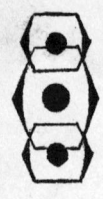

I read the Bible systematically for a short period every day. Often I have found that the verses have contained the wisdom or the assurance that I have needed for the problems of the day.

Sometimes I have been gripped by the direct and personal way in which the Bible has 'spoken' to me, so much so that the book has established itself in the pattern of my living as an indispensable 'must'.

I remember an occasion when I was interviewing one of the senior officials of my department who carried considerable responsibilities. He was on the verge of a nervous breakdown by reason of anxieties connected with his work, as well as domestic worry. After examining with him all the problems, and making provision for the relief he needed, I asked him if he would be interested to know the way I approached the responsibilities I carried as the corporation's Borough Engineer. He said that he would, and I told him much of what I have written in this article. Years later, after I had left that local authority for the service of another one, that officer wrote a letter to me, thanking me for sharing with him my experience about the Bible.

I would commend to everyone the thoughtful, regular reading of the Bible. It has an up-to-date message relevant to the times in which we live. The book is different from other books; it is alive, and the diligent reader will not have been reading it long before he finds for himself that this is so.

John Bunyan

Author of The Pilgrim's Progress

Read the Bible, and read it again, and do not despair of help to understand something of the will and mind of God, though you think they are fast locked up from you. Neither trouble yourself, though you have not commentaries and expositions; pray and read, and read and pray; for a little from God is better than a great deal from man; also what is from man is uncertain, and is often lost and tumbled over by man; but what is from God is fixed as a nail in a sure place.

There is nothing that so abides with us as what we receive from God; and the reason why Christians at this day are at such a loss as to some things is because they are content with what comes from men's mouths, without searching and kneeling before God to know of Him the truth of things. Things which we receive at God's hand come to us as things from the minting house, although old in themselves, yet new to us.

Old truths are always new to us, if they come to us with the smell of heaven upon them.

Air Vice Marshal Neil Cameron,
C.B.E., D.S.O., D.F.C.

The first time the Bible was really brought to life for me was one day in 1952 when I was lying in bed in St. George's Hospital, Hyde Park Corner, London, pretty low in spirits after a period of one and a half years in and out of hospital suffering from a most serious illness. I was visited by Captain Hartley-Holmes R.A. (retired) (completely unexpectedly for I had never met him before) who was then the Secretary of the Officers' Christian Union. (He died last year, after a life of dedication to God, aged 82). He left with me a New Testament which I still carry with me today, and consult each night even though it is now getting very tattered. In the fly-leaf he had written a text which is a favourite one:

'My soul, wait thou only upon God; for my expectation is from Him', and he also pointed out to me at that time of illness, another which I have never forgotten, Psalm 119:71, 'It is good for me that I have been afflicted; that I might learn thy statutes.'

These are but two examples of the comfort and support the Bible has given me during times of illness and stress. But that is not the complete picture. Since my recovery from illness the Bible has been a great companion in my service life in times of tension and often uncertainty or when some decision or other had to be made—then I turn to Admiral Jackie Fisher's favourite prayer: 'O lord in Thee do I put my trust let me never be confounded'.

Last but not least the New Testament story which more than any other has been a calming influence when the soul is troubled by some issue perhaps of service life, has been the post Resurrection journey to Emmaus as so beautifully told in St. Luke's Gospel, Chapter 24:13–33.

'And behold two of them went that same day to a village called Emmaus which was from Jerusalem about three score furlongs', and finishing. 'Did not our heart burn within us while He talked with us by the way and while He opened to us the scriptures.' Thank God the scriptures have been opened up to me in my life and service.

John H. Cordle

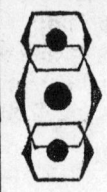

*Member of Parliament for Christchurch
and East Bournemouth*

I am very grateful to have this opportunity to say in a few words that the Bible means to me.

I am impressed by the authority of the Bible as I read it. He who made this book made me, for He knows me, and He knows all mankind. It does not idealise us all; in fact it says so many blunt things about human behaviour and human nature that are unpalatable because they are true.

This book has authority for me, and it brings comfort in tragedy, as I well know, as well as stern rebuke to self-indulgence. It is both comforting and uncomfortable. And I believe its principles are authoritative because they work. Some of them seem silly at first sight, e.g. 'Give, and it shall be given unto you' and 'Do as you would be done by'. And these principles are not only for a chosen minority; they will work for anyone whether Christian or not.

This book has a good deal to say about everyday life, some of it unacceptable until life has hit us hard, and we have been compelled to face our own failures and weakness.

And this book makes men to be brothers whatever national, social or cultural barriers may stand between.

The real difficulty is to make time to think about some little bit of it every day, and to apply it personally.

The Bible demands so much because it offers so much—comfort, peace, hope, joy, courage and much else that can transform life. It is indeed 'The most valuable thing that this world affords' (Quote from the Coronation service).

But the Bible is conditional: to get the full benefit of electric power we must keep the laws of electricity; to enjoy the Bible we must learn to obey it, and for some of us that's not easy—but I have seen it work.

Major-General A. J. H. Dove,
C.B., C.B.E.

On a January Sunday in 1924 a rather reluctant young officer was taken to an evangelistic meeting at a Soldiers' Home. I was that officer, and I came away from that meeting with a deep realisation that I was missing something in life, which I had not thought before had existed at all.

God was beginning to speak to me.

Two days later I found that I could not get away from a deep disquiet, and I lay down on my bed and opened my Bible at random. I started to read the first chapter of St. Paul's letter to the Romans, and I realised that God was describing my state. But what was the answer?

I read on, and as I reached the second chapter I came to a verse which sent me to my knees. Suddenly God had spoken, and through our Lord Jesus Christ, had met my need. I cannot now remember which verse it was, but I believe it was verse 4: 'Despisest thou the riches of His goodness and forbearance and longsuffering; not knowing that the goodness of God leadeth thee to repentance?'

But if the Bible could meet my need once ('Show me myself, and show me my Saviour'), it was certainly a book worth studying. And so as my duty took me to many parts of the world, in peace and in war, the Bible has travelled with me. Before the last war I was called to serve in Palestine, and how wonderfully interesting it was to see with my own eyes places which I had read about in its pages. The Bible came alive in a fresh way, with a conviction of its accuracy and authority.

And so, day by day, as I read my Bible, I find it gives me a yardstick by which to judge my life, and an inspiration that continues to throw light on the problems of daily living.

Professor J. W. Fairbairn
D.Sc., Ph.D., B.Sc., F.P.S.

My faith can be summed up as follows: 'I believe the Bible is the Word of God.' Not only does this imply that I believe in a Supreme Being but that He is a Personal God who is sufficiently interested in man to send us a written message. If this is true then it is a fact of staggering importance and demands the urgent attention of every thinking person.

Obviously God has chosen to use human channels to convey the message, often verbally, before committing it to writing. Now if a President Nixon has the power to communicate an important message to Mr. Kosygin so that the latter can pick up a paper in Russian and learn (within the limits of human language) exactly what Nixon's thoughts are, we cannot doubt it is beyond the wit of Almighty God to arrange that when I pick up my Bible I have exactly the same thoughts of God for me.

I am therefore unreservedly a Fundamentalist! And in this sense the Scientist is also fundamentalist because he must accept by faith certain fundamental assumptions. Firstly that there is a real world of facts outside us; secondly, that these facts are related by regular laws and thirdly, that our minds have the capacity to discover and understand these laws.

There is no logical proof for these assumptions. But if, for instance, his experiment this week gives a different result from the same one performed last week the scientist does not conclude that Nature's Laws have changed. Rather than doubt this Uniformity of Nature he would blame his experiments and enquire if some mistake there may not lead on to further knowledge. Such salutary humility reminds us of Paul's statement 'Let God be true and everyman a liar'.

So then, like more illustrious scientists before me, I study God's book of Nature, accepting its facts as the final authority, and as a Christian I study God's book of revelation accepting its statements and doctrines as the authoritative data on which to build my spiritual life. Alas! our generation has largely lost this balance, reading only Nature's book and forgetting Nature's God. Small wonder that the President of the U.S. National Academy of Sciences recently said that 'many of our young people are dismayed and sink into contemplation of the purpose-lessness of life'. Equally recently another American scientist refers to 'Science and Technology . . . the gods that failed'. How urgent then is the need of our scientifically biased generation to turn again to the claim that the Bible is the Word of God.

Dr. Billy Graham

The Bible is the most modern book in the world. It has been the anvil upon which the critics have worn out their hammers. Critics claim the Bible is full of forgery, fiction, and unfulfilled prophecy: but the findings of archaeology have corroborated rather than denied the Biblical data.

God's laws for the spiritual world are found in the Bible.

If you are setting up yourself as a critic, it is your responsibility to read and know both sides of the question. It is significant that very few Bible critics have bothered themselves to read the literature available on the defence of the Bible, much less the Bible itself.

'Has less knowledge of the Bible been accompanied by a breakdown in our moral fibre?' you ask. It certainly has. 'Will a return improve and raise the moral level of our people?' It certainly will! It has been proved time after time in our history. Robert E. Lee once said, 'The Bible is a book in comparison with which all others in my eyes are of minor importance, and which in all my perplexities and distresses has never failed to give me light and strength.'

The story of the Scriptures is the story of your redemption and mine through Jesus Christ. The Scriptures teach the death, burial, and resurrection of Christ.

JESUS CHRIST IS THE GOSPEL. And without Him you are lost and doomed.

The Bible teaches that there is a Hell and a Heaven.

The way to Heaven is by receiving and trusting Jesus Christ.

The Bible says 'All have sinned, and come short of the glory of God' (Romans 3:23). And the Bible also says, 'The soul that sinneth, it shall die' (Ezekiel 18:20). The Bible says that the only way the gap between man and God can be bridged is through Christ. Jesus said, 'I am the way, the truth, and the life: no man cometh into the Father, but by Me.'

Today you can accept the Christ of the Bible; you can know peace of soul, peace of conscience, and peace of mind by letting Him come into your heart by faith.

WILL YOU NOW, AS YOU READ THESE WORDS, OPEN YOUR HEART TO CHRIST?

Sir Kenneth Grubb,
K.C.M.G.

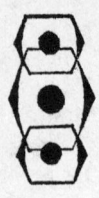

I have been a lover and reader of the Bible throughout life. The Bible has a word for all. Through it the mystic can seek union with the Divine Spirit as the author of all creation. To the Bible the most exacting theological mind must turn for fresh light to break forth on the full meaning of Christ's redemptive work. Those who yearn for the unity of mankind, not to say a closer union of Christians, will find their prayer taken up in the language and vision of the Bible. The prophetic souls, the great reformers, will read here the conditions of happiness, peace, and justice among the nations. The contemplative will dwell on the quiet pastures and the beauty and perfection of the life of the Good Shepherd. It supplies those simple and profound truths, those flashes of insight from the Holy Spirit of God, which can help us order our lives as Christians in business and profession, in leisure and home life. It calls upon both the thoughtful and the thoughtless to consider their ways and the ways of God with men. In hours of trial and loneliness it strengthens hope and faith and opens to us the vision of Eternal Life. For these reasons I have been a reader of the Bible for well over sixty years, for it speaks of the mighty acts of God in history, and of the life, death, and risen life of our Lord and Saviour Jesus Christ. Therefore, in every radical development of thought and life, I sought to consider what the Bible had to say.'

Admiral Sir John Hamilton,
G.B.E., C.B.

Dr William Temple wrote that 'the heart of religion is a personal relationship with God'. I have certainly found this to be true in my own life. In no sphere has this been more strikingly revealed than in one's attitude to the Bible. Until I came to a personal relationship with God, the Bible never really came alive and I had difficulty reading it regularly. But once I came to a personal relationship and learnt that the whole purpose of life was to do God's will, whatever one's profession or job, I found myself wanting to read the Bible. How could one do the will of somebody one did not know? How could one be guided by somebody with whom one was not in touch? It was natural to turn to the Bible to find out what God's will was, and to learn more of Christ's teaching.

I can only give it as my personal experience that since becoming a committed Christian I have found my daily Bible reading an essential part of my life. Moreover, I have found that the Holy Spirit helps to interpret it to each one of us individually so that its pages become alive and fruitful. The Bible is not a book of reference. Through its pages God speaks personally to each one of us.

To say that the Bible is not relevant to the problems of this scientific and technical age is to deny the very essence of our Christian faith, which is concerned with how we conduct ourselves in our homes, in our jobs, in our contacts with other people. Where else but in the Bible would the Christian find a way of life and a standard of conduct for every situation, based on the teaching and example of Christ? It is for neglect of this that the world and our own beloved country are in such a mess today.

George Frederick Handel

German born, naturalised citizen of England, Handel had an apoplexy stroke at the age of 52 on 13th April, 1737. He composed his masterpiece at the age of 56 in twenty-four days. In the rush of creative activity Handel composed nine operas between 1737 and 1741. In 1741 Queen Caroline, his staunch patroness, died, and his income was reduced. Weary, deeply in debt, inspirationless, he wandered through the dark London streets, seeking to avoid his creditors and crying in despair 'Why did God permit my resurrection, only to allow my fellow men to bury me again?' . . . 'My God, my God, why hast Thou forsaken me?'

Hopelessly he sought his lodgings in Brook Street. All were asleep. Slowly he climbed the stairs. A bulky parcel lay on his desk. Hastily breaking the seal he undid the wrappings, and found a libretto *A Sacred Oratorio* for which Charles Jennens wished him to compose the music. But Handel did not want a religious composition! He snuffed out his candle and went to bed—but not to sleep. Restless he arose to look at the manuscript—*Messiah*.

'Comfort ye'. The first words 'Comfort ye' arrested his attention. He turned the pages 'The people that walked in darkness . . . His Name shall be called Wonderful, Counsellor, the mighty God'. Heavenly portals seemed to open as harmonies flooded his soul. He read on, entranced 'Glory to God in the highest . . . then shall the eyes of the blind be opened . . . rest your souls . . . He was despised and rejected of men . . . He looked for some to take pity on Him, but there was no man.'

Realising a kinship of experience, he bowed his head in humility, then scanned the next page, 'Lift up your head . . . the Lord gave the Word . . . I know that my Redeemer liveth, . . . Rejoice.' Fires of genius burned in his soul. Mingling his tears with the ink, he rapidly jotted down notes. Melodies again filled his being. Strength returned till his pen was sometimes unable to keep pace with the flow of imagination. In almost superhuman activity he dashed through page after page of notes.

When his manservant brought his breakfast tray the next morning, he found Handel still bent over his desk. At noon when he returned, the food had not been touched. For three weeks Handel scarcely ate or slept. He wrote as intoxicated, jumped up, strumming on his harpsichord, flinging his arms in the air, singing at the top of his voice with tears streaming down his cheeks, 'Hallelujah! Hallelujah!'

'I think that I did see all heaven before me, and the great God Himself,' Handel afterwards explained. Time and space were obliterated as he sang and wrote in his artistic frenzy. The score of *Messiah* was finished on 14th September, 1741. He saw and heard no more, and fell on his bed exhausted. Handel slept as though in a coma for seventeen hours. His manservant who had received only vague answers, thought he was dying, and sent for Dr Jenkins who was away on a fishing trip. But before he arrived Handel was up, bellowing for food, and laughing uproariously 'You're possessed of the Devil, you know,' diagnosed the doctor. 'I think rather that God has visited me,' Handel countered.

Messiah is remarkable for its unity. Part I portrays the longing of the world for the Messiah and the announcement of His birth: Part II, the death and resurrection of Christ climaxing the triumphs of the Gospel in the 'Hallelujah Chorus', while Part III declares the doctrinal truths of faith in God, and assurance of immortality. An unbroken sequence is preserved throughout the fifty-three numbers, skilfully interspersed by aria, recitative and chorus.

Major K. Hedges,
M.B., Ch.B., D.T.M., R.A.M.C.

Major-general Sir Robert Ewbank, K.B.E., C.B., D.S.O., M.A. wrote a foreword to an article written by Major Hedges for *Practical Christianity*, the magazine of 'The Officers' Christian Union'.

Extract from foreword: 'Major Ken Hedges was the doctor on the four-man British Trans-Arctic Expedition which made the first ever surface crossing of the Arctic Ocean, and which was the first British party to reach the North Pole. This historic journey took 476 days and covered 3,620 route miles. This took place in 1969.

The following words were written by Major Hedges on the influence which the Bible had on him during that journey:

Often during our trek we would experience an almost inescapable sense of insignificance as we lived and moved in the vastness of an inhospitable and sometimes hostile environment. Yet I was to find that the Bible assured and re-assured me of my total significance to the straight claims and inescapable challenges of the Gospel of the Lord Jesus Christ. During the trek I was to have to learn a new and deepening respect for Holy Scripture:

 It warns all of us.

 It guides those who will read.

 It presents me with the Gospel of forgiveness and restoration.

 It provides the very means of starting and continuing in a purposeful relationship of trust in Christ.

Its own evidence proves that the Bible is nothing more

nor less than the Word of God. Indeed it was to be on Christmas Day that I was to read in Hebrews 4:12 'The Word of God is living and active, sharper than any two-edged sword, piercing to the division of soul and spirit, of joints and marrow, and discerning the thoughts and intentions of the heart.'

A Housewife with Children

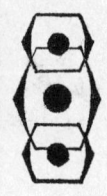

Every home must have foundation, and to me as a Christian housewife, that foundation must be the Bible. In this insecure, materialistic age, it is essential that a home should be based on the unchanging, and yet entirely relevant, Word of God.

I have found the Bible to be not only an inspired book, but an intensely practical and down-to-earth book, dealing with all the essentials of making the home secure and stable for its occupants—the loving relationship of husband and wife, the responsibility of bringing up a disciplined family, the giving of hospitality, the standard set for the ideal wife. All this and much more is to be found in God's Guide Book. Which of us does not experience days of frustration, crisis, anxiety, and difficulty in the best regulated of homes? How wonderful to be able to claim some of the promises from the Bible to help us through such days.

One of the joys of being a housewife is the unique opportunity one has in opening the home to neighbours and friends to come in for informal Bible study and chat. And if, as well as being a housewife, one is also a mother, surely the most wonderful privilege of all must be for her to train her children from babyhood to love the Bible stories, and to ground them in continuing years in the Scriptures.

If every housewife in our land made the Bible her Book of Rules for daily living, what a national transformation would occur.

Eric Hutchings

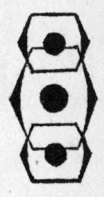

The well-known Evangelist

1 Without it I would be in the dark about certain facets of God's relationship with His people down the centuries.

2 Without its revelation I could not look for or explain the mystical working of the Holy Spirit convicting men to sin, bringing some to New Birth in Christ, giving gifts to the church and to individuals.

3 Without it I would not know that God, who, at sundry times, spoke in times past to the fathers by the prophets, has in these last days spoken to us by His Son the Lord Jesus Christ.

4 Without it I would not know that Christ died to put away my sin, and now risen from the dead, gives me the very life of God.

5 Without it I would be quite unable to explain the tragic deterioration in morality or find any answer to the survival of devilish demonic manifestation in so many individuals.

6 Without it I would be bewildered by the trend towards world climactic chaos and the prophesied hope of the return of the Lord Jesus to save the world from this fate; militarily, socially and ecologically.

7 Without it I would have no concept of eternal Salvation in the glories of Heaven.

A. L. Kensit

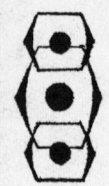

*Secretary of the Protestant Truth
Society and Leader of The Wickliffe
Preachers*

Many years ago a man I greatly admired when I was a young man, Mr. Hensman, the founder of The Berean Band, said:

> 'I love Thy Holy Word O Lord,
> Because it speaks of Thee,
> Reveals to me Thy Grace and Power,
> To cleanse my heart as hour by hour
> Thy love is shown to me.
>
> I hide within my heart Thy Word.
> From sin to set me free.
> It is a lamp to light my way
> To keep my feet as day by day
> I hide myself in Thee.'

In a very personal way I identify myself with these words.

But in my public ministry I have constantly in mind that I inherited a great name from my father and his father before him, and like them I have endeavoured by God's grace to uphold the great cause of the Protestant faith. With Luther I hold the evangelical doctrine of Justificaton by Faith alone; with Calvin the Sovereignty of God; with Cranmer, Latimer and Ridley, the Reformed Faith and practice of the Church of England as purged at the Reformation; and my authority for all this is found in God's Holy Word, The Bible. For instance it reminds me that the Holy Scripture contains all that is necessary to salvation (2 Tim. 3:15–17), that tradition is to be rejected (Matt. 15:1–3, 9), that Christ is the Head of the Church (1 Cor. 3:11), that there is no other mediator but Jesus Christ (1 Tim. 2:5), that images should not be worshipped (1 Cor. 6:9), that Christ died once; a complete sacrifice for sin and that therefore the Mass is a dangerous deceit (Heb. 10:14).

In a controversial work such as the Lord has called me into, one could give examples of many other points of false doctrine condemned in the sacred volume.

In stating briefly, therefore, what the Bible means to me let me say:

> It is my foundation on which to build.
> It is my food. Thy Words were found, and I did eat them (Jer. 15:16).
> It is my seed to be scattered (Luke 8:11).
> It is my comfort. Thy Word is a lamp unto my feet (Psalm 119:105).
> It is my joy. O how love I Thy law (Psalm 119:97).

I never cease to praise God for those who laid down their lives to give us, and preserve for us, His Book and pray that I may be kept faithful to proclaim its truths and the glorious message of the Gospel of His saving grace.

Admiral Sir Horace R. Law,
K.C.B., O.B.E., D.S.C.

Bible—Library, that is what the word means. A collection of books and, divided as it is into Old and New parts, they each tell of a different way and time of God's dealings with men.

The Old Testament is the history of the way God dealt with His chosen people and foreshadows the way in which He was going to deal with the world. There are many wonderful stories, and many places where the coming of Christ is foretold. And the setting up of sin offerings and sacrifes of animals, which is all carefully described in the Old Testament, show us the meaning of Christ's sacrifice made at Calvary and God's intention that His Son should replace fully all previous sacrifices and be the sin offering for ever.

But perhaps the most wonderful statement in the Old Testament are the verses in Genesis 1:26–27 in which it is stated and re-emphasised that God made man in His own image. God is a spirit and it is putting His Spirit into man that man can claim to be like God. It also means therefore that God is vitally interested in man, in each man, that is in you and me.

And then to the New Testament. The coming and work of Jesus Christ on earth, His crucifixion, death, and resurrection, all described in simple language by simple people, but in a way which makes it impossible, or at any rate unreasonable not to believe that it all happened.

And if we come to believe that Christ really did live, and die, and rise again, then we should not hesitate to come to Him and say, like Thomas did, 'My Lord and my God.'

We may then read on to learn about the first years of the Christian church, and how the Holy Spirit of God worked in men and women to transform them, and to give them the ability to spread the good news in spite of opposition.

Is it then just history? No, it is more than that, for God caused His servants to write for our learning and guidance and help, and He uses our reading of the Bible to teach and lead us in His way. Read what Paul wrote to Timothy in 2 Timothy 3:16–17 (N.E.B.) 'Every inspired scripture has its use for teaching the truth, refuting error, or for reformation of manners and discipline in right living, so that man who belongs to God may be efficient and equipped for good work of every kind.'

A Minister of the Gospel

To me the Bible is the inspired Word of the living God, the most wonderful book that has ever been written, unique in its comparison with all other literature. It has proved to me its truthfulness and reliability by its fulfilment of its many marvellous predictions which cannot be explained away by forgery or unbelief. Its many human writers, guided by the Spirit of God unite in their testimony to the majesty, holiness, and greatness of our God; great in His almighty power, and great in His amazing love.

It depicts down the centuries the troubles that come upon nations and individuals for rejecting the Word of God, and the sure deliverance which God grants, sometimes immediately, and always ultimately, to those who believe God's Word, and humble themselves before Him. It has lifted me up from a state of hopeless despair, and set my feet upon a rock, and has put a new song in my heart.

In the Bible I find food for my spiritual hunger, forgiveness and mercy for my many sins, comfort in my trials, a new Life in Christ Jesus, the Son of God, and a glorious hope for my future. This incomparable book reveals that all true love, all true joy, and all true peace come to men through its Divine Author, so that the neglect of it robs many people of untold blessings.

If its claim to be God's Word is true, as I firmly believe it to be, then the folly of rejecting its teaching can be clearly seen in the terrible state of society today, and in the solemn warnings God is continually giving to the world.

In the 'Gideon' Bible we find these words about the Bible 'It involves the highest responsibility, will reward the greatest labour, and condemns all who trifle with its sacred contents. Come to it with awe, read it with reverence frequently, slowly and prayerfully. It is given you in this life; it will be opened in the judgment, and is established for ever.'

The Venerable Archdeacon C. C. H. M. Morgan,

Q.H.C., M.A.

The Chaplain of the Fleet

There was a sudden quiet amongst those standing at the bedside. The great novelist, Sir Walter Scott, lay dying at Abbotsford, his lovely home on Tweed, surrounded by many of his friends. This was his hour of greatest need. As visibly he weakened, he turned slowly with the urgent request 'Pass me the Book!' Without delay one of his friends went to the desk in the window, fumbling vainly amongst the books on top—doubtless some were copies of the Waverley Novels—and asked 'Which Book?' Pointing to the Bible, Sir Walter Scott replied, 'There is only one Book!'

It is this uniqueness—'there is only one book'—expressed in the realm of human experience in the face of sorrow, disappointment, and even of death, that makes the Bible so remarkable.

In the Coronation Service there is a striking incident where the Archbishop of Canterbury, with the Moderator of the Church of Scotland, presents to the Sovereign a copy of the Scriptures, with the words 'We present you with this Book, the most valuable thing the world affords. Here is wisdom, this is the Royal Law, these are the lively oracles of God'.

To me the Bible is the 'one Book' that really meets the needs and demands of daily living. Not only does it claim to have a Divine authorship, but thousands of ordinary people, like ourselves, down the years have also proved its worth and testified to its uniqueness—its wisdom in times of uncertainty, its comfort in time of need, and its strength in time of weakness.

It is in the Bible that I personally find a source of continuous inspiration and encouragement. It records, with remarkable accuracy, events in the lives of men and women whose deeds and exploits, done in the name of God, still rivet the attention and capture the imagination. Men like Gideon with his 300 followers against the overwhelming might of the Midianites, the young David fearless in the face of Goliath, or another young man, Joshua, whose courage and determination led the Israelites to the Promised Land. These convince me of God's faithfulness at all times, of His power and ability, even in our difficult modern days, to fulfil what He has promised.

Above everything else, I find that in the Bible, unlike any other book I know, God speaks to me in clear and unmistakable ways. When faced with problems in my work or in my life, like the Psalmist, I, too, have found 'Thy Word is a lamp unto my feet, and a light unto my path'. Here is immediate help—like a storm lantern—light to enable me to take the next step now in safety; or like the far reaching sweep of the searchlight, light upon the distant scene of life.

Let God speak to you through its pages day by day, and you, too, will experience its uniqueness—'There is only one Book!'

Victor Pollard

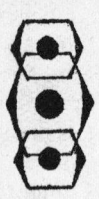

New Zealand Cricketer

At an early age I faced the most important decision of my life, and one which faces you. I had to decide whether I was going to accept or reject Jesus Christ as my Saviour and Lord. The Lord Jesus says, 'He that is not with Me is against Me.' I am overjoyed to tell you that I accepted Him, and, in the intervening period of eleven years, have never regretted my choice.

Can a true Christian be a true sportsman? This is the question I have faced. The impression gained by the youngster reading today's papers would be that sport offers you everything. They seem to read:

'Sport is most important. Devote yourself to it. Sport will bring you fame and renown.' Yes, but the Bible reads: 'Seek first the Kingdom of God and His righteousness and all these things shall be added unto you'; and also the Lord Jesus said 'I am the way, the truth, and the life'.

Sport has its place in life, as do business, family, home, pleasures, recreation, and many other things, but they are all so temporary. The Bible, in I Timothy 4:8, puts sport in its right perspective, 'For bodily exercise profiteth little (in contrast to much): but godliness is profitable unto all things, having promise of the life that now is, and of that which is to come.' God must come first and then all these things slip into place. The Lord Jesus told a parable about a rich man who was a successful farmer and then sat back in retirement. Then God said: 'Thou fool, this night thy soul shall be required of thee: then

whose shall those things be, which thou hast provided?'
(Luke 12).

This man never thought of God. After reading this we must ask ourselves individually, 'Am I rich toward God?' The man in the parable had left himself poor in the one area that counted for himself and counted in God's eyes. He had not learnt the value of 'Set your affection on things above, not on things on the earth' (Colossians 3:2).

As a cricketer I have been very fortunate. Two tours in England, India and Pakistan, and one in Australia and I am only twenty-three years of age. Yet to me, knowing Jesus Christ as my Saviour is a greater thrill than anything cricket can offer, or, in fact, than this world offers. To be in Christ's team, and have Him as Captain of my life is more wonderful to me than any national representation. How does one qualify for His team? Realise that you are a sinner, 'For all have sinned and come short of the Glory of God.' So you need forgiveness.

We read that 'He bore our sins in his body on the tree' and that 'If we confess our sins He is faithful and just to forgive us our sins'. So do just that, and then receive Him into your heart and life as your Saviour to carry you through, and as your Lord to obey. Finally, God loves you. Therefore seek Him diligently. Pray to Him constantly. Read His Word constantly. Remember Jesus Christ.

Cliff Richard

The Pop Star

I can confidently say that my favourite book is the Bible. When I was on tour in Australia with the Shads, I told Brian Locking, our lead guitarist, that I was thinking of going to a seance to 'get in touch' with my Dad, who had died the previous year. He was definitely against it; I asked him 'Why?'; and he simply said it was wrong and began to read bits of the Bible to me. I was really shaken to find one of my friends took the Bible so seriously. Not only that, but it seemed to make sense.

I decided to try reading it myself. I began with the Gospels, Matthew, Mark, Luke, and John, in the New Testament. I found it fantastically interesting. . . . As you read the New Testament you are forced to face up to a tremendously important question: 'Either Jesus Christ was a fool or a liar, or else He was what He said He was, the Son of God.'

. . . Once you come to grips with the Bible, you can't shake off its truth. But most people won't come to grips with it. The general attitude of ordinary people is to ridicule the Bible, to tear it to pieces and say it's full of contradictions, and so on. But most of them have never made a serious attempt to read it. . . . Christians have to keep on emphasising that the Bible is their authority. We must prove its worth, its inspiration, its authority and its truth.

Stan Smith

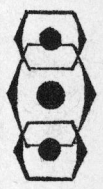

Wimbledon Lawn Tennis Champion 1972

The Bible is the most important book in my life. It was written centuries ago, but its contents are as relevant today, as ever before, if, indeed, not more so. The Bible covers every aspect of life; and in most instances it is interesting reading especially when using *The Living Bible* which is a paraphrase in today's language (without losing its vital meaning), but more importantly it contains the truths that Christ lived by and taught throughout His short but influential ministry. These truths give us guide-lines for every aspect of our lives. Today people are moving toward new morals. These are not really new, and they are not the answer for those seeking meaning in their lives. I meet many people who are wealthy and/or very liberal in their ideals. A good number of these people are not happy, their families are disjointed or separated, and their children don't know how to react to these evident problems that their folks have. The Bible speaks about family relationships, wife to husband, father and mother to children. The Bible speaks of happiness which is not found in money (Mark 8:36–38, also 1 Timothy 6:6–12, 17–21).

The step of accepting Christ as our Saviour, that He died for all our sins, and that we just have to make a commitment of faith, are all found in John's Gospel, and in the letter to the Romans, as well as other parts of the New Testament. One of my favourite verses is John 14:6 'Jesus said to him "I am the way, the truth, and the life; no one comes to the Father, but by Me".' I found

51

that the Bible did not have the full meaning for me until I took the step of faith. James 1:5-7 states that if faith is wavering prayers may not be answered. The writings in the Bible take on new significance with a strong faith in Christ.

I need to spend more time in studying the Bible. Bible Study Groups help one to learn and clarify its contents. I am always learning and am inspired constantly by what I read. I feel that God gives me guidance through the Scriptures and through prayer.

Dr. D. C. Spanner,
Ph.D., A.R.C.S., F.INST., BIOL.

Reader in Plant Physiology,
University of London

I think my attitude to the Bible can be best expressed in terms of what it means to me on three levels, the intellectual, the moral, and the spiritual.

These things correspond very roughly with the three things the prophet tells us the 'Lord requires of us' (Micah 6:8) as belonging to the good life. I will deal with them in turn.

Firstly, the intellectual attitude! What is it to be a man? Has life a meaning? Is history going anywhere? To these questions the Bible gives satisfying and challenging answers. Man is a created being, made in God's image, charged with the stewardship of the earth, and with an account one day to be rendered (Genesis 1:27–28; Acts 17:31). This wide-ranging view answers such diverse questions as to why human life seems so often tragically unfulfilled in rich and poor alike (Deuteronomy 8:3); whether it is right to pursue science and technology (Genesis 1:28); and what is the root from which springs man's pollution of his environment (Isaiah 24:5–6); all contemporary problems in our confused age.

Then, secondly, there is one's moral attitude to life. Is it really true that there are no absolute standards? Is everything relative, and must we for ever flounder in a morass of uncertainty? To these questions the Bible gives decisive answers, illustrated by its words about the immigrant (Deuteronomy 10:19), about industrial relations (Proverbs 21:3, 5, 6) and about the marriage bond (Malachi 2:14), all again very contemporary issues.

53

To me its answers are authoritative and convincing. I have purposely chosen them from the Old Testament; the New Testament goes even further. Lastly, there is the level of the spiritual.

The Bible makes this pre-eminent, for man it says was made for fellowship with God, and only in this does he find his real fulfilment, and become truly human. (Colossians 2:10; 1 John 1:3.) This is the most wonderful claim of all, and it is here that, more than anywhere else, the Bible authenticates itself as Divine revelation, God's Word to man's need. I must confess I revel in it. I read it every day, and rejoice as it illuminates the dark places of life, and brings me into a closer, more intelligent, and more filial relationship with God, through the Lord Jesus Christ.

His Honour Judge David Stinson

Chancellor-designate of the Diocese of Carlisle

On holiday this year, looking up at the star-studded vault of heaven, apparently infinitely vast and yet, as I believe, created by the will of God for his good purpose, I considered how small I am by comparison.

How does God in his infinite greatness make known his purpose to me, small as I am? In faith I believe that God the Holy Spirit, the Living God, uses the Bible to speak to me. Here I find Christ. Here I find the account of God's intervention in human history. Here I find the perfect life of the Son of Man, the perfect Sacrifice of Christ, the perfect power of the Resurrection and the perfect presence of the Holy Spirit. Here Paul makes clear how our fallen human nature has been crucified with Christ and that we have indeed been born again and are living in Christ—that eternal life in the Kingdom of God is here and now, if we will only accept it.

The Bible became compulsive reading for me at a time when I became conscious of my sins. A period of self-examination led me to confession and the overwhleming experience of the love and power and presence of Jesus Christ which brought me peace with God.

I receive personal and daily help from my Bible, relying on the scholarship of translators and commentators to help me. *The Living New Testament* and *Good News for Modern Man* are both translations in paperback which clarify the meaning in the beauty of the Authorised Version. *The Jerusalem Bible* presents both the Old and New Testaments in straight-forward modern English.

The Revised Standard Version is perhaps the best combination of intelligibility with memorable language.

The late Bishop Walter Carey used to advocate reading the Bible, starting with the Acts of the Apostles, and then reading the Gospels, and the Old Testament.

Dr. Frederick A. Tatford

Ph.D., Litt.D.

has held may high positions in the Civil Service, and was for some years a Director of the U.K. Atomic Energy uthority as well as being author and editor.

In a speech made during his term of office Mr. Harold Macmillan coined a phrase which has often been quoted since, when he referred to 'The wind of change'. A decade or two earlier, as Alexander Blok, the Russian poet, lay dying, he said, 'I can hear the storm winds of history blowing over my head'. If either man were to describe the conditions of the present day, he would probably refer, not to winds, but to tornadoes: so tempestuous and unrestrained are the metaphorical typhoons, which tear up our very foundations and create a basic uncertainty and insecurity which chill the heart of thinking man.

To what direction can we turn to discover what is yet to happen, and from whence can we derive help in these troubled days?

There is only one answer to questions of this nature. A revelation has been given of the future of man, and of the planet on which he lives. The veil has been drawn aside to reveal that there is a supreme throne on which sits the Governor of the universe, and to disclose that nothing takes Him unawares. His purpose has been decided from a past eternity, and His programme is unfolding precisely as He predicted.

That revelation is, of course, made in the Bible. The Scriptures are not merely a declaration of the character of God, and of the way of salvation for guilty man; they are also a disclosure of His predetermined plans for the universe, and I will never forget the thrill when I first discovered the extent of the Bible's unfolding of the future, and particularly the wealth of references to our Lord's coming for His people, and for the blessing of earth. That thrill has never left me. I turn to the Bible again and again, and on almost every page I find the predictions of the second Advent of the Saviour.

This book is the supreme guide to the future, and the outstanding inspiration of 'The blessed hope'.

Pastor Richard Wurmbrand

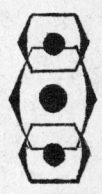

who suffered in prison under the Communists for many years and is now the Founder and leader of 'Christian Missions to the Communist World'

Bread does not mean the same thing for a millionaire as for a starving man. The Bible does not mean the same thing for a Christian of the Free world who may possess many different versions of the Scriptures, as for someone who lives behind the Iron Curtain, in a country where the Bible is a rarity. *The Sower*, organ of the Australian Bible Society, in its issue of September 1972, stated that for every thousand Bibles printed in the Free world, only one is taken to a person in a Communist country.

In the Free world one can buy and read a Bible easily, without facing any trouble. But in the Eastern Communist countries people are imprisoned for smuggling in Bibles or propagating its teachings.

For us Christians the Bible is primarily a manual for the spiritual warfare we are called upon to wage. We learn from it to look upon any compromise with sin and sinful institutions as cowardice and treachery. The Bible teaches us not to be unduly impressed by high titles. The Chief Priests were the people who sentenced our Lord Jesus to death. There are patriarchs and Protestant leaders in Communist countries who betray Christianity and denounce Christians to the Secret Police, with the result that many faithful Christians are put in prison. Forsaken by our religious leaders, we lean upon the Bible on our journey through the wilderness to our Heavenly home. It is again the Word of God which teaches us Christians how great are our privileges as the children of our Father in Heaven. It is the Bible which gives us deep confidence in all our conflicts. What real harm can our enemies do to us? We learn from the Scriptures that we never receive a blow which is not needful, and not one thorn that was not required to keep us from being exalted above measure. In Communist prisons, Bible verses memorised bring much comfort and strength. One remembers a Word of God, and with a promise from God one can face great discomfort with little food and sleep. Only by the indwelling Holy Spirit can such help as this be found. Lastly, the Bible gives us assured hope as to the final issue of this great conflict. God must have the last word; for our Lord Jesus Christ is yet going to be King over all the earth, and every knee shall yet bow to Him. Glory and praise be to our triumphant Saviour. Yes, I love the Bible.